T0016912

The Word became flesh
and made his dwelling among us.

JOHN 1:14 NIV

FROM
HEAVEN

A 28-Day Advent Devotional

A. W. TOZER

MOODY PUBLISHERS
CHICAGO

Edited by Kevin Emmert
Interior and cover design: Erik M. Peterson
Cover image of nativity copyright © by LinkCreative / Lightstock (188781).
All rights reserved.

Library of Congress Cataloging-in-Publication Data

Names: Tozer, A. W. (Aiden Wilson), 1897-1963, author.
Title: From heaven : a 28-day Advent devotional / A. W. Tozer.
Description: Chicago : Moody Publishers, 2016.
Identifiers: LCCN 2016021237 (print) | LCCN 2016023824 (ebook) | ISBN 9781600668029 | ISBN 9781600669033 ()
Subjects: LCSH: Advent--Meditations.
Classification: LCC BV40 .T69 2016 (print) | LCC BV40 (ebook) | DDC 242/.332--dc23
LC record available at https://lccn.loc.gov/2016021237

Paperback ISBN: 978-0-8024-3264-3

Originally delivered by fleets of horse-drawn wagons, the affordable paperbacks from D. L. Moody's publishing house resourced the church and served everyday people. Now, after more than 125 years of publishing and ministry, Moody Publishers' mission remains the same—even if our delivery systems have changed a bit. For more information on other books (and resources) created from a biblical perspective, go to www.moodypublishers.com or write to:

Moody Publishers
820 N. LaSalle Boulevard
Chicago, IL 60610

1 3 5 7 9 10 8 6 4 2

Printed in the United States of America

CONTENTS

Week 3

Week 4

A JOURNEY OF WAITING AND PREPARING

From Heaven is a collection of 28 daily readings from the beloved 20th-century pastor and writer A. W. Tozer (1897–1963). The selections have been gleaned from his recorded sermons—which have been edited for print—his published books, and his editorials while serving as editor of *The Alliance Witness* magazine (now *Alliance Life*). Each reflection has been carefully selected for the season of Advent.

Advent is the time of waiting and preparing for Christmas. From the Latin *adventus*, meaning "coming," Advent proclaims the coming of Christ in two ways: it celebrates His long-awaited arrival as Messiah, and it anticipates His return as King of kings and Lord of lords. In the Western church calendar, Advent begins on the fourth Sunday before Christmas, the Sunday closest to November 30, and lasts through Christmas Eve (December 24).

Common practices associated with Advent include lighting candles as a reminder that the Light has come to our dark world, keeping an Advent calendar, following prescribed Scripture readings and prayers, and reading daily devotionals. This devotional was compiled to help readers grow in their faith by reflecting on the wonder of the incarnation, the extent of God's love, and the hope for Christ's return. For each day, you will find one or more passages of Scripture included with each excerpt from Tozer. The editors of this volume suggest that the reader contemplate each devotional throughout the day and how it unpacks the truth of Scripture.

Advent does not always last for four full weeks each year, as the season can start any time between November 27 and December 3. So if you are using this book during a year when Advent is shorter than 28 days, consider combining multiple readings as needed in order to read through the entire volume.

As a result of reading these devotional selections, Tozer would want that each reader not simply learn more about God's work in Christ, but truly worship and serve God in awe and gratitude.

—THE EDITORS

Week 1

THE LOST PRESENCE

Then the man and his wife heard the sound of the
*L*ORD *God as he was walking in the garden in the cool*
of the day, and they hid from the L*ORD *God.*

GENESIS 3:8

. . . the Lord God banished him from the Garden of Eden . . .

GENESIS 3:23

The Word became flesh and made his dwelling among us.

JOHN 1:14

A dam had lost the presence of the Creator God and in the Bible record of the ages that followed, God never dwelt with men again in quite the same way.

To the Israelites, God dwelt in the Shekinah, hidden in the fire and the cloud. Occasionally He would appear in what theologians call a theophany, an appearance of the Deity. God might speak briefly with a man as He did with Abraham in the tent door or with Gideon on the threshing floor. God did not linger; His appearance always cautious and veiled.

Even when God showed Himself to Moses it was in the fire of the burning bush or while Moses was hidden in the cleft of the rock. The eyes of fallen, sinful men were no longer able to endure the radiant majesty and glory of Deity.

Then, in the fullness of time, He came again to men, for "And the Word was made flesh, and dwelt among us."

They called His name Immanuel, which means "God with us." In that first coming of Jesus the Christ, God again came to dwell with men in person.

I will have you know that I am not a prepositional preacher but at this point we must note three prepositions having to do with the coming of Jesus, God appearing as man.

He appeared to dwell *with* men. He appeared to be united *to* men. He came to ultimately dwell *in* men forever. So, it is with men, and to men, and in men that He came to dwell.

I always note with a little chuckle the frustrations of the translators when they come to such passages as "No man hath seen God at any time, the only begotten Son, which is in the bosom of the Father, he hath declared him" (John 1:18).

God's Word is just too big for the translators. They come to this phrase in the Greek: *The Son hath declared Him.* In the English of the King James Version it is just *declared.* In other versions they skirt it, they go around it, they plunge through it. They use two or three words and then they come back to one. They do everything to try to say what the Holy Ghost said, but they have to give up. Our English just will not say it all.

When we have used up our words and synonyms, we still have not said all that God revealed when He said: Nobody has ever seen God, but when Jesus Christ came He showed us what God is like (paraphrase of John 1:18).

I suppose that our simple and everyday language is as good as any.

"He has revealed Him—he has shown us what God is like!"

He has declared Him. He has set Him forth. He has revealed Him. In these ways the translators shift their language trying to get at this wondrous miracle of meaning.

But that man walking in Galilee was God acting like God. It was God, limited deliberately, having crossed the wide, mysterious gulf between God and not God; God and creature. No man had seen God at any time.

"The only begotten Son, which is in the bosom of the Father . . ." (John 1:18)—will you note that *was* is not the tense? Neither does it say that the Son *will be* in the Father's bosom. He *is* in the Father's bosom. It is stated in present, perpetual tense; the continuous tense, I think the grammarians call it. It is the language of continuation.

Therefore, when Jesus hung on the cross He did not leave the bosom of the Father.

You ask me, then: "Mr. Tozer, if that is true, why did our Lord Jesus cry out, 'My God, my God, why hast thou forsaken me?'" (Mark 15:34).

Was He frightened? Was He mistaken?

Never, never!

The answer should be very plain to us who love Him and serve Him.

BRIDGING THE GULF

The Word became flesh and made his dwelling among us.
We have seen his glory, the glory of the one and only Son,
who came from the Father . . .

JOHN 1:14

John the Baptist bears witness of Him, and cried saying, "This is He of whom I spake, He that cometh after me is preferred before me [that is, in honor]: for he was before me [that is, in rank]." And out of His fullness we have received grace following grace. The law was given by Moses, but grace and truth came from Jesus Christ. No man has seen God at any time, the only begotten Son, which is in the bosom of the Father, He hath declared Him.

We notice first of all that John said the Word became flesh, or the Word was made flesh. What we have here, stated in four words, is one of the darkest mysteries of human thought: How the Deity could cross the wide yawning gulf that separates what is God from what is not God. For in the universe there are really only two things: God and not God, that which is God and that which is not God. And all that is not God was made by God. And God was made by none. So we have God and not God. And the gulf that exists between God and not God—that is between the Creator and the creature, between the being we call God and all other beings—is a great and vast and yawning gulf. How God could bridge this—and how God could join the Creator to the creature—constitutes one of the profoundest and darkest mysteries to which human thought can ever give itself.

If you have never thought very much about this, it may not seem so amazing. But if you have given it a little thought, you will see how astonishing it is that the unbridgeable gulf between God and not God—for the very archangels and the seraphim and the cherub that shield stones of fire are not God, so that there is a gulf fixed, a vast gulf, a gulf of infinitude—and how God managed to bridge that and how He could join Himself to His creatures, and how He could limit the limitless, or in the language we hear more popularly, how the infinite could ever become the finite. And how that which had no limit, which is God, should deliberately impose upon Himself limitations. And how God and why God would favor one order of being above another.

If you read your Bible you will discover that man is not the only order of being. Man, in his sinful pride, thinks he is. We do not even believe in angels anymore. We think angels are simply Santa Clauses with wings, and Protestants do not believe in angels anymore. Foolishly we do not believe in angels. Nor do we believe in cherubim or seraphim or watchers or holy ones or any of these strange principalities and powers that walk so darkly bright through the passages of the Bible. We do not believe them as much as we should at any rate. And yet they are there, and mankind is only one order of God's being of creatures.

How and why God should favor one above the other? For it is written in the book of Hebrews that God took upon Him not the nature of angels, but He took upon Him the seed of Abraham. Abraham certainly was not equal to an angel. One would suppose that God in stepping down should step down as little as He dared or could, that He would stop with an angel or a seraphim, but instead He came down to the lowest order, and took upon Himself the nature of Abraham, the seed of Abraham.

Even that man Paul, who was declared to be one of the six greatest intellects of all time, that great man of God, threw up his hands and said, "Great is the mystery of godliness."

GOD MANIFESTED IN FLESH

The Word became flesh and made his dwelling among us . . .
full of grace and truth.

JOHN 1:14

Christ Jesus is not only Redeemer, but the Sustainer, the Creator, the Upholder, the One who holds all things together, the adhesive quality of the universe. To those who believe, Christ Jesus is the medium through whom God dispenses grace to all of His creatures, including those to be redeemed and those who do not need to be redeemed.

It is true that there are orders upon orders and ranks upon ranks of creatures that do not need to be redeemed.

Yet, it is also true, that they live by grace as well as the lowest sinner who is converted.

Through the apostle John, the Holy Spirit tells us that the eternal Son, the Word who became flesh, is full of grace and truth.

Let us remember this: everything God does is by grace, for no man, no creature, no being deserves anything. Salvation is by grace, the creation is by grace—all that God does is by grace and every human being has received of His fullness.

This boundless grace must operate wherever that which is not God appeals to that which is God; wherever the voice of the creature crosses the vast gulf to the ears of the Creator.

How do the angels get their broad wings?

Out of His grace.

How do the principalities and powers, the ranks and the columns of shining creatures appearing through the pages of the Bible get what they have?

Out of His grace upon grace.

I dare to ask in this context: What have you received of His grace and mercy?

Even though you may still be unconverted and going your own way, you have received much out of the ocean of His fullness. You have received the pulsing life that beats in your bosom. You have received the brilliant mind and brain within the protective covering of your skull. You have received a memory that strings the events you cherish and love as a jeweler strings pearls into a necklace and keeps them for you as long as you live and beyond.

All that you have is out of His grace. Jesus Christ, the eternal Word, who became flesh and dwelt among us, is the open channel through which God moves to provide all the benefits He gives to saints and sinners.

And what about the years, the rest of your existence?

You cannot believe that you have earned it.

You cannot believe that it has something to do with whether you are good or bad.

Confess that it is out of His grace, for the entire universe is the beneficiary of God's grace and goodness.

WHAT THE ADVENT ESTABLISHED

. . . he made himself nothing by taking the very nature of a servant, being made in human likeness . . .

PHILIPPIANS 2:7

T he birth of Christ told the world something: that He should come to be born of a woman, to make Himself of no reputation and, being found in fashion as a man, to humble Himself even to death on a cross— this is a fact so meaningful, so eloquent as to elude even the power of a David or an Isaiah fully to celebrate. His coming, I repeat, told the world something; it declared something, established something. What was it?

That something was several things, and as Christ broke the loaves into pieces for greater convenience in eating, let me divide the message into parts the easier to understand it. The advent established:

First, that God is real. The heavens were opened and another world than this came into view. A message came from beyond the familiar world of nature. "Glory to God in the highest," chanted the celestial host, "and on earth peace, good will." Earth the shepherds know too well; now they hear from God and heaven above. Our earthly world and the world above blend into one scene and in their joyous excitement the shepherds can but imperfectly distinguish the one from the other.

It is little wonder that they went in haste to see Him who had come from above. To them God was no longer a hope, a desire that He might be. He was real.

Second, human life is essentially spiritual. With the emergence into human flesh of the Eternal Word of the Father, the fact of man's divine origin is confirmed. God could not incarnate Himself in a being wholly flesh or even essentially flesh. For God and man to unite they must be to some degree like each other. It had to be so.

The incarnation may indeed raise some questions, but it answers many more. The ones it raises are speculative; the ones it settles are deeply moral and vastly important to the souls of men. Man's creation in the image and likeness of God is one question it settles by affirming it positively. The advent proves it to be a literal fact.

Third, God indeed spoke by the prophets. The priests and scribes who were versed in the Scriptures could inform the troubled Herod that the Christ was to be born in Bethlehem of Judaea. And thereafter the Old Testament came alive in Christ. It was as if Moses and David and Isaiah and Jeremiah and all the minor prophets hovered around Him, guiding His footsteps into the way of the prophetic Scriptures.

So difficult was the Old Testament gamut the Messiah must run to validate His claims that the possibility of anyone's being able to do it seemed utterly remote; yet Jesus did it, as a comparison of the Old Testament with the New will demonstrate. His coming confirmed the veracity of the Old Testament Scriptures, even as those Scriptures confirmed the soundness of His own claims.

Fourth, man is lost but not abandoned. The coming of Christ to the world tells us both of these things.

Had men not been lost, no Savior would have been required. Had they been abandoned, no Savior would have come. But He came, and it is now established that God has a concern for men. Though we have sinned away every shred of merit, still He has not forsaken us. "For the Son of man is come to seek and to save that which was lost."

Fifth, the human race will not be exterminated. That which was God seized upon that which was man. "God of the substance of His Father, begotten before all ages; Man of the substance of His mother, born in the world. Perfect God and perfect Man . . . who, although He be God and man, yet He is not two but one Christ." God did not visit the race to rescue it; in Christ He took human nature unto Himself, and now He is one of us.

For this reason we may be certain that mankind will not be wiped out by a nuclear explosion or turned into subhuman monsters by the effects of radiation on the human genetic processes. Christ did not take upon Himself the nature of a race soon to be extinct.

Sixth, this world is not the end. Christ spoke with cheerful certainty of the world to come. He reported on things He had seen and heard in heaven and told of the many mansions awaiting us. We are made for two worlds and as surely as we now inhabit the one we shall also inhabit the other.

Seventh, death will some day be abolished and life and immortality hold sway. "For this purpose the Son of God was manifested, that he might destroy the works of the devil," and what more terrible work has the devil accomplished than to bring sin to the world and death by sin? But life is now made manifest by the appearing of our Savior Jesus Christ, who hath abolished death and hath brought life and immortality to light through the gospel.

THE MEANING OF CHRISTMAS

. . . He appeared in the flesh . . .

1 TIMOTHY 3:16

So completely are we carried away by the excitement of this midwinter festival that we are apt to forget that its romantic appeal is the least significant thing about it. The theology of Christmas too easily gets lost under the gay wrappings, yet apart from its theological meaning it really has none at all. A half dozen doctrinally sound carols serve to keep alive the great deep truth of the incarnation, but aside from these, popular Christmas music is void of any real lasting truth. The English mouse that was not even stirring, the German Tannenbaum so fair and lovely, and the American red-nosed reindeer that has nothing to recommend it have pretty well taken over in Christmas poetry and song. These along with merry old St. Nicholas have about displaced Christian theology.

We must not forget that the church is the custodian of a truth so grave and urgent that its importance cannot be overemphasized, and so vast and incomprehensible that even an apostle did not try to explain it; rather it burst forth from him as an astonished exclamation:

> And without controversy great is the mystery
> of godliness: God was manifest in the flesh,
> justified in the Spirit, seen of angels, preached
> unto the Gentiles, believed on in the world,
> received up into glory.
> I TIMOTHY 3:16

This is what the church is trying to say to mankind but her voice these days is thin and weak and scarcely heard amid the commercialized clangor of "Silent Night."

It does seem strange that so many persons become excited about Christmas and so few stop to inquire into its meaning; but I suppose this odd phenomenon is quite in harmony with our unfortunate human habit of magnifying trivialities and ignoring matters of greatest import. The same man who will check his tires and consult his road map with utmost care before starting on a journey may travel for a lifetime on the way that knows no return and never once pause to ask whether or not he is headed in the right direction.

The Christmas message, when stripped of its pagan overtones, is relatively simple: God is come to earth in the form of man. Around this one dogma the whole question of meaning revolves. God did come or He did not; He is come or He is not, and the vast accumulation of sentimental notions and romantic practices that go to make up our modern Christmas cannot give evidence on one side or the other.

Certain religious teachers in apostolic times refused to believe that Jesus was actually God come in the flesh. They were willing to exhaust the language of unctuous flattery to describe His glorious manhood, but they would have none of His deity. Their basic philosophy forbade them to believe that there could ever be a union of God and human flesh. Matter, they said, is essentially evil. God, who is impeccably holy, could never allow Himself contact with evil. Human flesh is matter; therefore, God is not come in the flesh.

Certainly it would not be difficult to refute this negative teaching. One would only need to demonstrate the error of the major premise, the essential sinfulness of matter, and the whole thing would collapse. But that would be to match reason against reason and take the mystery of godliness out of the realm of faith and make of it merely another religious philosophy. Then we would have rationalism with a thin Christian veneer. How long before the veneer wore off and we had only rationalism?

While faith contains an element of reason, it is essentially moral rather than intellectual. In the New Testament unbelief is a sin, and this could not be so if belief were no more than a verdict based upon evidence. There is nothing unreasonable about the Christian message, but its appeal is not primarily to reason. At a specific time in a certain place God became flesh, but the transcendence of Christ over the human conscience is not historic; it is intimate, direct, and personal.

Christ's coming to Bethlehem's manger was in harmony with the primary fact of His secret presence in the world in preincarnate times as the Light that lighteth every man. The sum of the New Testament teaching about this is that Christ's claims are self-validating and will be rejected only by those who love evil. Whenever Christ is preached in the power of the Spirit, a judgment seat is erected and each hearer stands to be judged by his response to the message. His moral responsibility is not to a lesson in religious history but to the divine Person who now confronts him.

LUKEWARM ABOUT CHRIST'S RETURN

Listen, I tell you a mystery: We will not all sleep,
but we will all be changed—in a flash, in the twinkling of
an eye, at the last trumpet. For the trumpet will sound, the
dead will be raised imperishable, and we will be changed.

1 CORINTHIANS 15:51–52

T he return of Christ as a blessed hope is, as I have said, all but dead among us. The truth touching the second advent, where it is presented today, is for the most part either academic or political. The joyful personal element is altogether missing. Where are they who

"Yearn for the sign, O Christ, of thy fulfilling,
Faint for the flaming of Thine advent feet"?

The longing to see Christ that burned in the breasts of those first Christians seems to have burned itself out. All we have left are the ashes. It is precisely the "yearning" and the "fainting" for the return of Christ that has distinguished the personal hope from the theological one. Mere acquaintance with correct doctrine is a poor substitute for Christ and familiarity with New Testament eschatology will never take the place of a love-inflamed desire to look on His face.

If the tender yearning is gone from the advent hope today there must be a reason for it; and I think I know what it is, or what they are, for there are a number of them. One is simply that popular fundamentalist theology has emphasized the utility of the cross rather than the beauty of the One who died on it. The saved man's relation to Christ has been made contractual instead of personal. The "work" of Christ has been stressed until it has eclipsed the person of Christ. Substitution has been allowed to supersede identification. What He did for me seems to be more important than what He is to me. Redemption is seen as an across-the-counter transaction, which we "accept," and the whole thing lacks emotional content. We must love someone very much to stay awake and long for his coming, and that may explain the absence of power in the advent hope even among those who still believe in it.

Another reason for the absence of real yearning for

Christ's return is that Christians are so comfortable
in this world that they have little desire to leave it. For
those leaders who set the pace of religion and determine
its content and quality, Christianity has become of late
remarkably lucrative. The streets of gold do not have too
great an appeal for those who find it so easy to pile up
gold and silver in the service of the Lord here on earth.
We all want to reserve the hope of heaven as a kind of
insurance against the day of death, but as long as, we are
healthy and comfortable, why change a familiar good for
something about which we actually know very little?
So reasons the carnal mind, and so subtly that we are
scarcely aware of it.

Again, in these times religion has become jolly good
fun right here in this present world, and what's the hurry
about heaven anyway? Christianity, contrary to what some
had thought is another and higher form of entertainment.
Christ has done all the suffering. He has shed all the tears
and carried all the crosses; we have but to enjoy the benefits
of His heartbreak in the form of religious pleasures
modeled after the world but carried on in the name of
Jesus. So say the same people who claim to believe in
Christ's second coming.

History reveals that times of suffering for the Church
have also been times of looking upward. Tribulation has
always sobered God's people and encouraged them to
look for and yearn after the return of their Lord. Our

present preoccupation with this world may be a warning of bitter days to come. God will wean us from the earth some way—the easy way if possible, the hard way if necessary. It is up to us.

TAKING UP HUMANITY

Since the children have flesh and blood,
he too shared in their humanity . . .

HEBREWS 2:14

John Wesley pointed out that it is a dark mystery how God could swoop down and become man and bridge the yawning gulf and join Himself to flesh and limit the limitless. Wesley also said that we should distinguish the act from the method by which the act was performed, and not reject a fact because we do not know how it was done.

I think that is very wise, and it would be very becoming to us if we should enter the presence of God, reverently bowing our heads, and singing carols and saying, "That it is so God, but we don't know how. We will not reject the fact because we do not know the operation by which it was brought to pass."

Now, this much we can know: the incarnation required no compromise of Deity. The gods of the Roman pantheon, the gods of Greece, and the gods of the Scandinavian regions were gods that would compromise themselves. The old Valhalla was full of gods that were compromisers, and the Elysian Fields and the Pantheon and all that—wherever the gods were, they always were gods who had to compromise themselves one way or another.

But the holy God—who is God, and all else not God— that God, our Father who art in heaven, could never compromise Himself. So that the incarnation—this deep, dark, yawning mystery—was wrought and accomplished without any compromise of the Deity. God did not degrade Himself by this condescension. He did not in any sense make Himself to be less than God. He remained God, and everything else remained not God. The gulf still existed even after Jesus Christ had become man and had dwelt among us. So that instead of God degrading Himself when He became man, He by the act of incarnation elevated mankind to Himself. He did not degrade Himself to mankind. That's pointed out very carefully in one of the old creeds, the Athanasian Creed. The old church fathers were very cautious here, and they would not allow us to believe that God, when He became flesh, became flesh by a coming down of the Deity into flesh, but by a taking up of mankind unto God. And thus we do not degrade God, but we elevate man, and that is the wonder of redemption.

Now we can know this again: that this unison or union with man and God is effected under perpetuity. God can never back out of His bargain. God can never cease to be, in that sense, man. The second Person of the Trinity can never un-incarnate or de-incarnate Himself. He became incarnated forever. The Word became flesh and dwelt among us.

Week 2

LIGHT FOR THE DARKNESS

Your word is a lamp for my feet, a light on my path.

PSALM 119:105

This revelation of Jesus Christ has to do with His relationship to the Father, to the human race, and to the church. It has to do with His relationship to Israel, to the nations, to our enemy the devil, and to the coming judgment.

Ministers faithful to the Word of God have always said that Christ can be found on every page of the Bible. In the Revelation, we see Him dominating the eternal future. The message of the book is the almost overwhelming portrayal of Christ's victory, bringing about the final destruction of Satan and all of his works.

Part of our Christian restfulness comes from the fact

that we are in the hands of a loving God who has already
existed throughout all of the tomorrows. Because all time
is in God, the flow of time never concerns God. He never
has to run in an effort to catch up with the movement of
time. The end of time is seen by God just as easily as the
beginning of time.

That is why the Bible tells us that God knows the
end from the beginning. That is why a godly man like
John, caught up in the Spirit of God, could be shown the
outline of future events. They were future to him, and
they are future to us. That is because we are in the stream
of time. They are not future to God because He is not in
the stream of time.

Revelation is the only New Testament book that may
be classified as "predictive" in its character and content.
(It has been interesting to me to find in the writings
of Blaise Pascal, the great 17th-century scientist and
religious philosopher, his conclusion that no true
prediction of mankind's future can be found anywhere
but in the Christian Scriptures.)

About the predictive quality of the Scriptures we
ought to be in agreement. If there cannot be any valid
foresight, no revelation from God, nothing to warn us
or prepare us for tomorrow, this life on earth would have
to be considered a gloomy business indeed. Thankfully,
we have a definite word, a promise upon which we can
lean. Peter, one of God's special spokesmen, expressed
it this way:

We have also a more sure word of prophecy;
whereunto ye do well that ye take heed, as
unto a light that shineth in a dark place, until
the day dawn, and the day star arise in your
hearts: Knowing this first, that no prophecy of
the scripture is of any private interpretation.
For the prophecy came not in old time by the
will of man: but holy men of God spake as they
were moved by the Holy Ghost.

2 PETER 1:19−21

As Christian believers, we are assured that no matter
how dark it becomes around us, God will faithfully provide the illumination of His Spirit. The Old Testament
offers in the release of Israel from Egyptian bondage a
fitting illustration. When God was moving toward the
climax of that deliverance, the darkness of night covered
Egypt, but, miraculously, there was light in the dwellings
of all of the Israelites. So, too, there is light even now for
us who are Christian believers concerning our future.
God's Word is a light that shines in a dark place until the
morning star rises in our hearts.

THE REDEMPTIVE PLAN

He came to that which was his own,
but his own did not receive him.

JOHN 1:11

I n earlier verses in John's gospel record, we have read in
remarkably brief and simple words of the eternal past
and of the eternal Son. We are told that from the beginning
He was God; that He made all things, and that in Him
was light and that in Him was life.

Surely, these powerfully simple words and phrases are
at the root of all theology. They are at the root of all truth.

How thrilling it is for us, then, to receive in these two
words, *He came,* the confirmation of the incarnation, God
come in the flesh!

I confess that I am struck with the wonder and the
significance of the limitless meaning of these two words,

He came. Within them the whole scope of divine mercy and redeeming love is outlined.

All of the mercy God is capable of showing, all of the redeeming grace that He could pour from His heart, all of the love and pity that God is capable of feeling— all of these are at least suggested here in the message that *He came!*

Beyond that, all of the hopes and longings and aspirations, all of the dreams of immortality that lie in the human breast, all had their fulfillment in the coming to earth of Jesus, the Christ and Redeemer.

Man has always been a hopeful creature, causing Milton to write that "hope springs eternal in the human breast." Even fallen man continues to be an aspiring creature. We are reminded that while mired in the pigsty, the prodigal remembered his father's house, and within himself pondered the question of "What am I doing here?"

All of our hopes and dreams of immortality, our fond visions of a life to come, are summed up in these simple words in the Bible record: *He came!* I suppose it is the editor nature within me to note that I am impressed with the fact that these two one-syllable words occupy only seven spaces in a printed line. But what these two words tell us is more profound than all of philosophy, and I am not using the superlative carelessly in this context.

There are times when the use of the superlative is absolutely necessary and you cannot escape it. The coming of Jesus Christ into this world represents a truth more profound than all of philosophy, for all of the great thinkers of the world together could never produce anything that could even remotely approach the wonder and the profundity disclosed in the message of these words, *He came!*

These words are wiser than all learning. Understood in their high spiritual context, they are more beautiful than all art, more eloquent than all oratory, more lyric and moving than all music—because they tell us that all of mankind, sitting in darkness, has been visited by the Light of the world!

Oh, I am sure that we are all too passive about what this really means! When we sing "The Light of the world is Jesus," there should be a glow on our faces that would make the world believe that we mean it.

OUR ANTICIPATION: JESUS THE VICTOR

*The kingdom of the world has become
the kingdom of our Lord and of his Messiah,
and he will reign for ever and ever.*

REVELATION 11:15

The unbeliever, who boastfully will "take my chances," can only remain cynical. Deep within, he or she discovers doubts and uncertainties multiplying daily. Tell that person about this revelation, about the certainty of Jesus Christ's ultimate victory, of God's promise of new heavens and a new earth, and he or she can only react with the cynic's biting contempt: "Who cares about fables and empty promises? No person in his right mind would ever confess that he has been reading the book of Revelation!"

Take my word for it. Men and women who think they have all the answers about this life and the next have been mouthing their brave words for generations. They are big, challenging words, but they come from puny, empty hearts and minds. These infidels are too blind to recognize or acknowledge that God does have an eternal plan—a divine plan in which mankind is never permitted to utter the first word or the last.

The fact is that God has always been God—and He always will be God. He knows all about our human beginnings. He has had to consult with no one about anything!

One day that little bundle of delight, so fondly nurtured by parents and family, finds herself in human consciousness and accepts the fact that she is. It is at that point that her volitional life begins. Until that time, she had nothing to say about anything—absolutely nothing.

Have you noticed, in the human family, how encouraged we are by the sound of our own voice? Men and women take to strutting and boasting, and in their pride they may declare their independence of God. Little do they realize that God in His divine sovereignty has reserved the right to take up at the last where He began at the first. It can mean only one thing: human beings are in the hands of God finally, whether they will or not.

I declare this truth in all frankness because God's Word, including the book of Revelation, tells us clearly that our man-made civilizations, so called, will not prevail in the coming day of judgment and consummation.

Secular-minded men and women seem annoyed by the premise that the Creator-God has in mind a plan for ending this age in which we live. They do not want to be told that organizations, governments, and institutions cannot expect earthly things to continue as they are for ever and ever. Repeatedly and plainly the Bible tells us to expect Jesus, the Christ of God, to return to this earth in power and glory. People who have long joked about the "invisibility" of the kingdom of God will see it established in righteousness and with authority.

Humans try to ignore God, continuing to make their own ambitious, selfish plans. In the years before World War I, Germany's Kaiser Wilhelm, largely blamed for the beginning of that first world conflict, was exceedingly headstrong. At a chapel service attended by the kaiser, a faithful German minister preached on the coming again of Jesus Christ to establish God's kingdom of righteousness and peace throughout the earth. Wilhelm was greatly offended and spoke to the minister at the close of the service.

"I never want to hear that kind of a sermon again," he warned the preacher. "Such an event is not at all in keeping with the plans we have for the future and the glory of our Fatherland!"

But Kaiser Wilhelm and, a generation later, Adolf Hitler are merely fading memories—illustrations of that vain human propensity to make ourselves big and God small.

There is vastly more in Revelation than you or I will ever know while we are on this earth. But just God's urging that we be ready for the announced coming events should be sufficient to keep us expectant, interested—and praying!

THE LOGIC OF THE INCARNATION

Beyond all question, the mystery from which
true godliness springs is great: He appeared in the flesh.

I TIMOTHY 3:16

Probably no other doctrine in the entire Word of God carries in it greater difficulties than the doctrine of the incarnation. Paul called it the "mystery of godliness," and later writers either passed over its difficulties without trying to explain them or else involved the whole thing in a maze of explanations that offered little real help to an understanding of it. And we can easily see why this is so.

The incarnation brings to us the essential mystery of being. It touches almost every phase of human thought and makes demands upon philosophy and metaphysics, as well as upon theology. The great doctors have felt this deep mystery whenever they have come to the consideration of the subject and have tiptoed along the borders of it with deepest reverence. That is proper and right; such an attitude well becomes us who are but dust and ashes.

At the risk of being charged with inexcusable boldness, we venture the assertion that while the incarnation is mysterious, it is not illogical or contrary to reason. We would not presume to settle with a pen stroke those profound and awful mysteries that have stilled the voices of the ages and brought men and angels to their knees in worship; but we would dare to say that in our opinion the act of becoming man was altogether reasonable from God's standpoint. It placed no strain upon the divine nature and admitted into the scheme of God nothing unnatural or inconsistent. The reasons for so believing are these:

Man was originally made in the image of God. "God created man; in the likeness of God made he him." This is a cardinal doctrine of the Christian faith. It is not necessary to understand all that is included in this doctrine, for even here we run into some real theological problems. But faith can soar where reason can never climb, and it is only necessary that we believe the truth. Its power over us depends upon our believing it, not upon our understanding it. The fact is all that matters: man was made in the image of God.

Now, if man was made in the image of God, then God must certainly carry something of the image of man. (That sin has marred the image and introduced a foreign and destructive element into human nature does not detract from the force of the argument.) If a boy looks like his father, it must surely follow that the father must look like the boy. Somewhere within man's nature, twisted and deformed as it may be, there is godlikeness. This will not be seriously questioned by anyone who knows his Bible. No student of Christian theology would deny this as a fact, though he might reject the conclusions we draw from the fact.

If in the infinite condescension of God, mankind was made with a nature somewhat like its Creator, then is it not reasonable that God could clothe Himself with human nature in the mystery of incarnation, and all within the framework of easy possibility without the embarrassment of uniting things unlike each other?

When the ancient Word stood up in human flesh, He felt at home. He was not out of His element, for had He not heard the Father say, "Let us make man in our image, after our likeness"? There was no jar, no wrench caused by the forced union of dissimilar natures.

It is our humble opinion that the "exile" element in the earthly experience of our Lord has been greatly over-played. That He was sad and lonely and far from home, a stranger in a strange land, is an idea that has grown up around the beautiful and simple fact, but it is not necessarily a part of the fact. So far as we can recall there is nothing in the record to give the impression that His presence in human flesh was an unnatural or painful experience. He happily called Himself "the Son of Man," not an exile among men.

All this is not to attempt to take away from the valid mystery that surrounds the incarnation or to lessen the awe with which we contemplate the wonder of the Word becoming flesh to dwell among us. It is rather to clear away unauthorized notions and give the beauty of the incarnation a chance to make its own impression upon us. That impression will be deep enough without our adding anything to it.

CHRIST CAME FOR ALL

For God did not send his Son into the world to condemn the world, but to save the world through him.

JOHN 3:17

When the Word says that God sent His Son into the world, it is not talking to us merely about the world as geography. It does not just indicate to us that God sent His Son into the Near East, that He sent Him to Bethlehem in Palestine.

He came to Bethlehem, certainly. He did come to that little land that lies between the seas. But this message does not have any geographical or astronomical meaning. It has nothing to do with kilometers and distances and continents and mountains and towns.

What it really means is that God sent His Son into the

human race. When it speaks of the world here, it does not mean that God just loved our geography. It does not mean that God so loved the snowcapped mountains or the sun-kissed meadows or the flowing streams or the great peaks of the north.

God may love all of these. I think He does. You cannot read the book of Job or the Psalms without knowing that God is in love with the world He made. But that is not the meaning in this passage. God sent His Son to the human race. He came to people. This is something we must never forget: Jesus Christ came to seek and to save people. Not just certain favored people. Not just certain kinds of people. Not just people in general.

We humans do have a tendency to use generic terms and general terms and pretty soon we become just scientific in our outlook. Let us cast that outlook aside and confess that God loved each of us in a special kind of way so that His Son came into and unto and upon the people of the world—and He even became one of those people!

If you could imagine yourself to be like Puck and able to draw a ring around the earth in forty winks, just think of the kinds of people you would see all at once. You would see the crippled and the blind and the leprous. You would see the fat, the lean, the tall, and the short. You would see the dirty and the clean. You would see some walking safely along the avenues with no fear of a policeman but you would see also those who skulk in back alleys and crawl through broken windows. You would see those who are healthy and you would see others twitching and twisting in the last agonies of death. You would see the ignorant and the illiterate as well as those gathered under the elms in some college town, nurturing deep dreams of great poems or plays or books to astonish and delight the world.

People! You would see the millions of people: people whose eyes slant differently from yours and people whose hair is not like your hair.

Their customs are not the same as yours, their habits are not the same. But they are all people. The thing is, their differences are all external. Their similarities are all within their natures. Their differences have to do with customs and habits. Their likeness has to do with nature.

Brethren, let us treasure this: God sent His Son to the people. He is the people's Savior. Jesus Christ came to give life and hope to people like your family and like mine.

The Savior of the world knows the true value and worth of every living soul. He pays no attention to status or human honor or class. Our Lord knows nothing about this status business that everyone talks about.

When Jesus came to this world, He never asked anyone, "What is your IQ?" He never asked people whether or not they were well traveled. Let us thank God that

He sent Him—and that He came! Both of those things are true. They are not contradictory. God sent Him as Savior! Christ, the Son, came to seek and to save! He came because He was sent and He came because His great heart urged Him and compelled Him to come.

CHRIST—THE CHANNEL OF GRACE

For the law was given by Moses, but grace and truth came by Jesus Christ.

JOHN 1:17

The idea that the Old Testament is a book of law and the New Testament a book of grace is based on a completely false theory.

There is certainly as much about grace and mercy and love in the Old Testament as there is in the New. There is more about hell, more about judgment and the fury of God burning with fire upon sinful men in the New Testament than in the Old.

If you want excoriating, flagellating language that skins and blisters and burns, do not go back to Jeremiah and the old prophets—hear the words of Jesus Christ!

Oh, how often do we need to say it: the God of the Old Testament is the God of the New Testament. The Father in the Old Testament is the Father in the New Testament.

Furthermore, the Christ who was made flesh to dwell among us is the Christ who walked through all of the pages of the Old Testament.

Was it the law that forgave David when he had committed his great sins? No, it was grace displayed in the Old Testament.

Was it grace that said, "Babylon is fallen, the great harlot is fallen, Babylon is fallen" (paraphrase of Revelation 18:2)? No, it was law expressed in the New Testament.

Surely there is not this great difference and contrast between Old and New Testaments that many seem to assume. God never pits the Father against the Son. He never pits the Old Testament against the New.

The only contrast here is between all that Moses could do and all that Jesus Christ can do. The Law was given by Moses—that was all that Moses could do. Moses was not the channel through which God dispensed His grace.

God chose His only begotten Son as the channel for His grace and truth, for John witnesses that grace and truth came by Jesus Christ.

All that Moses could do was to command righteousness. In contrast, only Jesus Christ produces righteousness.

All that Moses could do was to forbid us to sin. In contrast, Jesus Christ came to save us from sin.

Moses could not save, but Jesus Christ is both Lord and Savior.

Grace came through Jesus Christ before Mary wept in the manger stall in Bethlehem.

It was the grace of God in Christ that saved the human race from extinction when our first parents sinned in the garden.

It was the grace of God in Jesus Christ yet to be born that saved the eight persons when the flood covered the earth.

It was the grace of God in Jesus Christ yet to be born but existing in preincarnation glory that forgave David when he sinned, that forgave Abraham when he lied. It was the grace of God that enabled Abraham to pray God down to ten when He was threatening to destroy Sodom.

God forgave Israel time and time again. It was the grace of God in Christ prior to the incarnation that made God say, "I have risen early in the morning and stretched out my hands unto you!"

The apostle John speaks for all of us also when he writes of the eternal Son and reminds us that *we beheld His glory.*

LET US PREPARE NOW

*Therefore keep watch, because you do not know
the day or the hour.*

MATTHEW 25:13

I t was John Milton who said that hope springs eternal in the human breast. Indeed hope is such a vital thing that were it to die out of the heart of mankind, the burden of life could not long be sustained.

But precious as this hope may be, it is yet, when it is ill-founded, a dangerous thing. The hope, for instance, which almost all people feel, of long life here on earth, can be for many a deadly snare, a fatal delusion. The average man, when he thinks of his future, suspends reason, falls back on unreasoning hope, and creates for himself an expectation of peaceful and unnumbered days yet to come. This blind optimism works all right till the last day, that inevitable last day that comes to all; then it betrays its victim into the pit from which there is no escape.

The perils of groundless hope threaten the Christian too. James sharply rebuked the believers of his day for presumptuously assuming an earthly future they had no real assurance would be theirs:

> Go to now, ye that say, To day or to morrow we will go into such a city, and continue there a year, and buy and sell, and get gain: Whereas ye know not what shall be on the morrow. For what is your life? It is even a vapour, that appeareth for a little time, and then vanisheth away. For that ye ought to say, If the Lord will, we shall live, and do this, or that. But now ye rejoice in your boastings: all such rejoicing is evil.
> JAMES 4:13−16

Would it not be good for us to put away the vain dream of countless earthly days and face up to the blunt fact that our days on earth may actually not be many?

For the true church, there is always the possibility that Christ may return. Some good and serious souls hold this to be more than a possibility, for it seems to them as it seems to this writer that "the earth is grown old and the

66

judgment is near," and the voices of the holy prophets are sounding in our ears.

And when He comes, there will not be a moment's notice, not an added day or hour in which to make frantic last-minute preparations.

> And take heed to yourselves, lest at any time
> your hearts be overcharged with surfeiting, and
> drunkenness, and cares of this life, and so that
> day come upon you unawares. For as a snare
> shall it come on all them that dwell on the face
> of the whole earth. Watch ye therefore, and
> pray always, that ye may be accounted worthy
> to escape all these things that shall come to
> pass, and to stand before the Son of man.
> LUKE 21:34–36

Altogether apart from the prophetic expectations of devout men, there is the familiar fact of death itself. Of those Christians who had died, Paul said simply, "Some are fallen asleep" (1 Corinthians 15:6). What a vast and goodly company they make, those sleeping saints, and how their number will be increased this year. And which ones among us can give assurance that he may not join them before all the days of the year have run their course?

Since we know not what a day may bring forth, does it not appear to be the part of wisdom to live each day as if it were to be the last? Any preparation we will wish we had made, let us make it now. Anything we will wish we had done, let us do it today. Any gift we will wish we had made, let us make it while time is on our side.

At the great unveiling, there will be other emotions beside joy. There will be grief and shock and self-reproach and disillusionment. But it need not be so for you and me if we will but use the information we have at hand, if we will but take advantage of the opportunities that lie beside our pathway and the promises that jut like uncut diamonds from the sacred Scripture. Yesterday may have been marked by shameful failure, prayerlessness, backsliding. Today all that can be changed and tomorrow— if there is for us an earthly tomorrow—can be filled with purity and power and radiant, fruitful service. The big thing is to be sure we are not lulled to sleep by a false hope, that we do not waste our time dreaming about days that are not to be ours. The main thing is to make *today* serve us by getting ready for any possible tomorrow. Then whether we live or die, whether we toil on in the shadow or rise to meet the returning Christ, all will be well.

Week 3

THE GLORY OF CHRIST

We have seen his glory, the glory of the one and only Son,
who came from the Father . . .

JOHN 1:14

I hear sermons on the radio sometimes that make the physical body everything, and works of miracle everything, and I wish that I could go along with such interpretations and say that the glory of Jesus Christ lay in His ability to cast out devils, heal the sick, raise the dead, and still the waves. Now undoubtedly that was wonderful, and He did get some praise to Himself from these necessary miracles. But I believe that there was a greater glory than merely works of wonder, which our Lord manifested there.

For always remember this friends, that who a man *is* is always more important to God than what he does. Remember that if a man were able to stand up and create pine trees and lakes and hills, but were not a good man, he would still be of no value to God. And let us remember that if a man were a good man, through and through a good man, and had no power at all to do any miracle, he would still be one of the sweetest treasures of God, and God would write his name on His own hands. For it is goodness that God is looking for; it is being and character and personality that God is looking for, not the ability to do amazing things.

So it was who Jesus was that was glorious, not only what He did. In fact, what He did was secondary; who He *was* was primary. So Jesus Christ's glory lay in the fact that He was perfect love in a loveless world, that He was purity in an impure world, that He was meekness in a harsh and quarrelsome world, that He evinced humility in a world where every man was seeking his own place, that He showed boundless, fathomless mercy in a hard and cruel world, that He evinced selfless goodness in a world full of selfishness. It was the deathless devotion of Jesus—and the patient suffering and the unquenchable life and the grace and the truth—that they beheld.

They beheld His glory, the glory of the only begotten Son from the Father, full of grace and truth. And so it was this that made Jesus wonderful. As little as the poor, blind world knows about it today in all its wild, money-inspired and profit-inspired celebrations, it is not celebrating turning water into wine. It is not celebrating healing the sick or raising the dead. It is not celebrating the cursing of fig trees or the sticking on of cut-off ears. The poor, blind world with what little bit of religious instinct it has left in it yet, is this season celebrating who He was.

JUST AS HE WENT

And when the Chief Shepherd appears, you will receive the crown of glory that will never fade away.

I PETER 5:4

Many new cults have arisen; men have walked through the streets saying, "I am Christ." The psychiatrists have written reams and reams of case histories of men who insisted that they were Jesus Christ.

But our Lord Jesus Christ has not yet appeared the second time, for if He had, it would have been consistent with the meaning of the word as it was commonly used in the New Testament. He would have to appear as He appeared in the temple, as He appeared by the Jordan or on the Mount of Transfiguration. It would have to be as He once appeared to His disciples after the resurrection—in visible, human manifestation, having dimension so He could be identified by the human eye and ear and touch.

If the word *appearing* is going to mean what it universally means, the appearing of Jesus Christ has to be very much the same as His appearing on the earth the first time, nearly 2,000 years ago.

When He came the first time, He walked among men. He took babies in His arms. He healed the sick and the afflicted and the lame. He blessed people, ate with them, and walked among them, and the Scriptures tell us that when He appears again He will appear in the same manner. He will be a man again, though a glorified man! He will be a man who can be identified, the same Jesus as He went away.

We must also speak here of the testimonies of Christian saints through the years—of Christ being known to us in spiritual life and understanding and experience.

There is a certain sense in which everyone who has a pure heart "looks upon" God.

There are bound to be those who will say, "Jesus is so real to me that I have seen Him!"

I know what you mean and I thank God for it—that God has illuminated the eyes of your spiritual understanding—and you have seen Him in that sense. "Blessed are the pure in heart, for they shall see God."

I believe that it is entirely possible for eyes of our faith, the understanding of our spirit, to be so illuminated that we can gaze upon our Lord—perhaps veiled, perhaps not as clearly as in that day to come, but the eyes of our heart see Him!

So, Christ does appear to people in that context. He appears when we pray and we can sense His presence. But that is not what Peter meant in respect to His second appearing upon the earth. Peter's language of that event calls for a shining forth, a revelation, a sudden coming, a visible appearance!

Peter meant the same kind of appearance that the newspapers noted in the appearance of the president of the United States in Chicago. He meant the same kind of appearance that the newspapers noted when the young sergeant appeared suddenly to the delight of his family after having been away for more than two years. There has not been any appearance of Jesus like that since He appeared to put away sins by the sacrifice of Himself!

We can sum this up and say that there is to be an appearance—in person, on earth, according to Peter—to believing persons later than Peter's time. That appearing has not yet occurred and Peter's words are still valid.

We may, therefore, expect Jesus Christ again to appear on earth to living persons as He first appeared.

WHAT WE HAVE RECEIVED

Out of his fullness we have all received grace
in place of grace already given.

JOHN 1:16

The Bible teaches so clearly and so consistently what John proclaims in the first chapter of his gospel: "And of his fullness have all we received, and grace for grace" (John 1:16).

Out of His fullness we have received. There is no way that it can mean that any of us have received all of His fullness. It means that Jesus Christ, the eternal Son, is the only medium through which God dispenses His benefits to His creation.

Because Jesus Christ is the eternal Son, because He is of the eternal generation and equal with the Father as pertaining to His substance, His eternity, His love, His power, His grace, His goodness, and all of the attributes of deity, He is the channel through which God dispenses all His blessing.

If you could ask the deer that goes quietly down to the edge of the lake for a refreshing drink, "Have you received of the fullness of the lake?" the answer would be: "Yes and no. I am full from the lake but I have not received from the fullness of the lake. I did not drink the lake. I only drank what I could hold of the lake."

And so, of His fullness, out of the fullness of God, He has given us grace upon grace according to our need, and it is all through Jesus Christ, our Lord. When He speaks, when He provides, while He sustains, it is because it can be said that He upholds all things by the word of His power and in Him all things consist.

Now, here is a thought I had one day: it could have been very easy for God to have loved us and never told us. God could have been merciful toward us and never revealed it. We know that among humans it is possible for us to feel deeply and still tell no one. It is possible to have fine intentions and never make them known to anyone.

The Scriptures say that "no man hath seen God at any time, the only begotten Son, which is in the bosom of the Father, he hath declared him" (John 1:18).

The eternal Son came to tell us what the silence never told us.

He came to tell us what not even Moses could tell us.

He came to tell us and to show us that God loves us and that He constantly cares for us.

He came to tell us that God has a gracious plan and that He is carrying out that plan.

Before it is all finished and consummated, there will be a multitude that no man can number, redeemed, out of every tongue and tribe and nation.

That is what He has told us about the Father God. He has set Him forth. He has revealed Him—His being, His love, His mercy, His grace, His redemptive intention, His saving intention.

He has declared it all. He has given us grace upon grace. Now we have only to turn and believe and accept and take and follow. All is ours if we will receive because *the Word was made flesh, and dwelt among us!*

TRUSTING IN GOD'S SOVEREIGNTY

He who testifies to these things says, "Yes, I am coming soon." Amen. Come, Lord Jesus.

REVELATION 22:20

Have you ever heard of a person eagerly reading an interesting book, then suddenly deciding to abandon it without reading the last chapter? The last chapter ties together the threads of the narrative; it summarizes the arguments; it climaxes the action. You and I would agree that to close a book without reading the final chapter would be to read without purpose and without satisfaction.

I have had people tell me that although they read the Bible, they stop short of Revelation—the final "chapter." Imagine! That particular Bible book announces itself as the revelation of Jesus Christ. It forecasts the consummation of all things and introduces the new order. How can readers form a balanced understanding of God, sin, unbelief, and divine judgment if they ignore so important a book? In these crisis days of world government, no Christian can afford to ignore the climactic Revelation.

We may take one of only two stances in regard to this prophetic "unveiling"—this portraying of the future return of Jesus Christ to this earth, to this world that once rejected Him as Messiah and crucified Him at Calvary. We may ignore it, in effect despising it and jeering at the prospect of a future divine intervention affecting the entire world. Or we may embrace it, cheering for the promised victory of a righteous Ruler, the coming King of kings.

Those who ignore Revelation take their place with the many who believe a humanistic view of life is sufficient: that men and women are responsible captains of their own souls. They take their place with the defiant multitude who shout the age-old refrain: "We will not have this Man to rule over us!"

Those who take Revelation seriously are convinced of an actual heavenly realm as real as the world we now inhabit. They are persuaded that the day of consummation nears when "the kingdom of the world" becomes "the kingdom of our Lord, and of his Christ," who "shall reign for ever and ever" (Revelation 11:15).

Living in this generation, we are fully aware that the competitive world and our selfish society have brought many new fears to the human race. I can empathize with those troubled beings who lie awake at night worrying about the possible destruction of the race through some evil, misguided use of the world's store of nuclear weapons. The tragedy is that they have lost all sense of the sovereignty of God! I, too, would not sleep well if I could not trust moment by moment in God's sovereignty and omnipotence and in His grace, mercy, and faithfulness.

The prevailing attitudes of fear, distrust, and unrest permeating our world are known to all of us. But in God's plan some of us also know a beautiful opposite: the faith and assurance found in the church of Jesus Christ. God still has a restful "family" in His church. As believers we gladly place our confidence in God's revelation of Himself. Although the material world has never understood our faith, it is well placed in the Scriptures. The Bible tells us many things we could learn in no other way.

This amazing Revelation—the final section of the holy Scriptures—tells us plainly that no human being and no world government or power will have any control or any say in that fiery day of judgment yet to come upon the earth. John's vision of things to come tells us clearly and openly that at the appropriate time the direction and administration of this world will be taken away from men and women and placed in the hands of the only Man who has the wisdom and power to rightly govern. That Man is the eternal Son of God, our Lord Jesus Christ.

Revelation describes the age-ending heavenly and

earthly events when our Lord and Savior is universally acknowledged to be King of kings and Lord of lords. All will acclaim Him victor. God's Revelation leaves us with no doubt about that.

In our present period of time, however, there is little recognition of God's sovereignty or of His plan for His redeemed people. Go into the marketplace, into our educational institutions, and—yes—even into our popular religious circles, and you will find a growing tendency to make mankind large and to make God small. Human society is now taking it for granted that if God indeed exists, He has become our servant, meekly waiting upon us for our will.

In the face of this kind of human thinking, I want to make a case for the committed Christians in this world. We are the true realists. We confess that we do not hold the powers of life and death in our own hands. We have sensed the importance of John's vision in the Revelation. We are assured that God is alive and well and that He has never abdicated His throne. While others may wonder and speculate concerning God's place in the universe, we are assured that He has never yielded to any of His creatures His divine rights as Lord of man and nature.

It is for this reason that the Christian believer, related to God by faith, is assured of final victory. Even in the midst of earthly trials, he or she is joyful.

DAY 19

THE REASONS HE CAME

For God did not send his Son into the world to condemn the world, but to save the world through him.

JOHN 3:17

Let us think and imagine ourselves back to the condition of paganism. Let us imagine that we have no Bible and no hymn book and that these 2,000 years of Christian teaching and tradition had never taken place. We are on our own, humanly speaking.

Suddenly, someone arrives with a proclamation: "God is sending His Son into the human race. He is coming!"

What would be the first thing that we would think of? What would our hearts and consciences tell us immediately? We would run for the trees and rocks and hide like Adam among the trees of the garden.

What would be the logical mission upon which God would send His Son into the world? We know what our nature is and we know that God knows all about us and He is sending His Son to face us.

Why would the Son of God come to our race?

Our own hearts—sin and darkness and deception and moral disease—tell us what His mission should be. The sin we cannot deny tells us that He might have come to judge the world!

Why did the Holy Ghost bring this proclamation and word from God that "God did not send his Son into the world to condemn the world" (John 3:17)?

Men and women are condemned in their own hearts because they know that if the Righteous One is coming, then we ought to be sentenced.

But God had a greater and far more gracious purpose— He came that sinful men might be saved. The loving mission of our Lord Jesus Christ was not to condemn but to forgive and reclaim.

Why did He come to men and not to fallen angels? Well, I have said this before in this pulpit, and I could be right, although many seem to think that because others are not saying it I must be wrong: I believe He came to men and not to angels because man at the first was created in the image of God and angels were not. I believe He came to fallen Adam's brood and not to fallen devils because the fallen brood of Adam had once borne the very image of God.

Thus, I believe it was a morally logical decision that when Jesus Christ became incarnate it was in the flesh and body of a man because God had made man in His image.

I believe that although man was fallen and lost and on his way to hell, he still had a capacity and potential that made the incarnation possible, so that God Almighty could pull up the blankets of human flesh around His ears and become a Man to walk among men.

There was nothing of like kind among angels and fallen creatures—so He came not to condemn but to reclaim and to restore and to regenerate.

CHRISTMAS REFORMATION LONG OVERDUE

. . . the Son of Man did not come to be served, but to serve . . .

MATTHEW 20:28

Christmas as it is celebrated today is badly in need of a radical reformation. What was at first a spontaneous expression of an innocent pleasure has been carried to inordinate excess. In one section of Chicago, for instance, the excited citizenry vie with each other each year for the biggest, gaudiest, and most vulgar Christmas tree, on the porch, on the lawn, along the street; and one gigantic, flashily dressed and cold but determinedly smiling Santa

Claus drives a fully lighted herd of reindeer across the yard and over the house!

How far have we come in the corruption of our tastes from the reverence of the simple shepherds, the chant of the angels, and the beauty of the heavenly host! The star of Bethlehem could not lead a wise man to Christ today; it could not be distinguished amid the millions of artificial lights hung aloft on Main Street by the Merchants Association. No angels could sing loudly enough to make themselves heard above the raucous, ear-splitting rendition of "Silent Night" meant to draw customers to the neighborhood stores.

In our mad materialism we have turned beauty into ashes, prostituted every normal emotion, and made merchandise of the holiest gift the world ever knew. Christ came to bring peace and we celebrate His coming by making peace impossible for six weeks of each year. Not peace but tension, fatigue, and irritation rule the Christmas season. He came to free us of debt and many respond by going deep into debt each year to buy enervating luxuries for people who do not appreciate them. He came to help the poor and we heap gifts upon those who do not need them. The simple token given out of love has been displaced by expensive presents given because we have been caught in a squeeze and don't know how to back out of it. Not the beauty of the Lord our God is found in such a situation, but the ugliness and deformity of human sin.

Among the harmful abuses of the Christmas season in America is the substitution of Santa Claus for Christ as the chief object of popular interest, especially among the children.

The morality of Mother Goose stories and fairy tales has been questioned by serious-minded Christian parents, but my opinion is that these are relatively harmless because they are told as fiction and the child is fully aware that they are imaginary. With Santa Claus it is not so. The child is taught falsehood as sober truth and is thus grossly deceived during the most sensitive and formative period of his life.

What shall we do? Cultivate humility and frugality. Put the emphasis where the Bible puts it, on the Christ at the right hand of God, not on the babe in the manger. Return to the simplicity that is in Christ. Cleanse our churches of the unscriptural pageantry borrowed from Rome. Take the Scriptures as our guide and refuse to be pressured into conformity to paganism practiced in the name of Christ.

JESUS—THE JUDGE OF HUMANITY

When the Son of Man comes in his glory, and all the angels with him, he will sit on his glorious throne. All the nations will be gathered before him and he will separate the people from one another as a shepherd separates the sheep from the goats. He will put the sheep on his right and the goats on his left.

MATTHEW 25:31–33

What is your concept of Jesus Christ, my brother? If the "ten-cent-store Jesus" that is being preached by a lot of men, the plastic, painted Christ who has no spine and no justice and is pictured as a soft and pliable friend to everybody—if He is the only Christ there is, then we might as well close our books and bar our doors, and make a bakery or garage out of this church!

But that Christ that is being preached and pictured is not the Christ of God, nor the Christ of the Bible, nor the Christ we must deal with.

The Christ we must deal with has eyes as a flame of fire, and His feet are like burnished brass, and out of His mouth comes a sharp, two-edged sword.

He will be the judge of mankind. And, thank God, you can leave your loved ones who have died in His hands, knowing that He Himself suffered, knowing that He knows all, that no mistakes can be made, that there can be no miscarriage of justice, because He knows all that can be known!

This is one of the neglected Bible doctrines of our day—that Jesus Christ is the judge of mankind.

The Father judges no man. When the Lord, the Son of Man, shall come in the clouds of glory, then shall be gathered unto Him the nations, and He shall separate them.

God has given Him judgment, authority, to judge mankind, so that He is both the Judge and Saviour of men.

That makes me both love Him and fear Him! I love Him because He is my Saviour and I fear Him because He is my Judge.

Human justice does its best, but because it is not all-wise it makes mistakes.

But God Almighty is never going to judge the race of mankind and allow a mistake to enter. The judge must be one who has all wisdom.

Therefore, I appeal away from St. Paul; I appeal away from Moses and Elijah; I appeal away from all men because no man knows me well enough to judge me, finally. And I don't know you well enough to judge you, finally.

I may pass brief judgment upon you on some simple matter, or you on me, but when it comes to the placing of my eternal and everlasting soul somewhere, I don't want any mistakes made.

To be a judge, according to the Scriptures, the judge considers those who are accountable to Him, and accountable to Him not by a law imposed by another, but accountable to Him morally and vitally, rather than merely legally.

And in order to be a righteous judge of mankind, the judge has to have all knowledge so there can be no error.

In human affairs, many an innocent man has been hanged. Many a "life-termer" has died in gray pallor behind prison walls while the rascal who actually committed the crime died in his own bed, surrounded by his friends.

Week 4

THREE TRUTHS BEHIND CHRISTMAS

But you, Bethlehem, in the land of Judah,
are by no means least among the rulers of Judah;
for out of you will come a ruler
who will shepherd my people Israel.

MATTHEW 2:6

Now the second chapter of Matthew gives us the story of the birth of the infant Lord. This story is the wonder story of all lands and all ages. It is also told by Luke. It is said to be, and I believe it is, the most beautiful story in human language. It is beautiful but terrible as well. For there are three unexpressed facts that explain the chapter, facts that are not here but that explain it. They are the setting for the chapter. They are that which go before and go after and make it intelligible to our intelligent minds.

There are these three things:

The total moral and spiritual disaster that had engulfed the human race. Now we cannot think of the coming of our Savior to the world apart from this, or think of a rescue ship going out to rescue those who had not been shipwrecked, or a doctor sent to a place where there had been no accident or epidemic.

This was a rescue. And that is the second unexpressed fact here. This is the story of a rescue, not a rescue team, of *one who came alone to rescue mankind and thus fulfill God's ancient purpose in sovereign grace, the sending of a Rescuer. Save* is the word we use and it means the same thing: *to save the world and to redeem men who had been caught in this disaster and engulfed in this woe.*

And the third is *the black malice, the cold fury of the one we call Satan, the destroyer.* You and I, all we human beings, we are adept at the business of presenting one side of a question. And all through this rather happy Christmas season, there is but one side presented: it is the side of the golden bells and the angels who said, "Peace on earth, good will to men." But I say these unexpressed facts make all this intelligible to mortal men. The evil, the fury loosed against humankind and through humankind against God. For it was not the devil's fury or anger at mankind that caused him to be the devil he is, but it was his anger with God. And since mankind was made in the image of God, and God has expressed—and did express—His great love for mankind, then it was to get at God that the devil attacked that race of beings that God had loved the most.

And so we have in this chapter—and I want you to think of the entire chapter, not just one text out of it—events that are solemn and fearful and breathtaking. We have a view of life inside and outside, a view of the human race, of the religious world and of the irreligious world, of the Jewish world and of the pagan world, of the temple and of the armory, of the priest and of the soldier, all here. And we have this view of yesterday and an explanation of today and a preview of tomorrow.

LIVING IN BETWEEN

. . . we wait for the blessed hope—the appearing of the
glory of our great God and Savior, Jesus Christ, who
gave himself for us to redeem us from all wickedness
and to purify for himself a people that are his
very own, eager to do what is good.

TITUS 2:13–14

Russia and the United States, the two great nuclear
powers, continue to measure their ability to destroy
in terms of *overkill.* This is a terrible compound word
never before used in the history of the English language.
The scientists had to express the almost incredible
destructive power of the nuclear bombs in our stockpiles—so the word *overkill* is a new invention of our times.

Both the United States and Russia have made statements about the overkill power of nuclear stockpiles sufficient to kill every man, woman, and child in the world—not once, but twenty times over. That is overkill!

Isn't it just like that old enemy, Satan, to persuade the saints in the body of Christ to engage in bitter arguments about posttribulation rapture and pretribulation rapture; postmillennialism, amillennialism and pre-millennialism—right at the very hour when overkill hangs over us like a black, threatening cloud.

Brethren, this is the kind of age and hour when the Lord's people should be so alert to the hope and promise of His coming that they should get up every morning just like a child on Christmas morning—eager and believing that it should be today!

Instead of that kind of expectancy, what do we find throughout His church today? Arguments pro and con about His coming, about the details of the rapture—and some of this to the point of bitterness. Otherwise, we find great segments of Christians who seem to be able to blithely ignore the whole matter of the return of Jesus Christ.

Very few ministers bother to preach from the book of Revelation any more—and that is true of large areas of evangelicalism and fundamentalism, too! We have been intimidated by the cynicism and sophistication of our day.

There are so many apparent anomalies and contradictions in society and in the ranks of professing Christians that someone will certainly write a book about it.

There is the anomaly of the necessity of getting to know one another better in order to love and understand one another better. Millions are traveling and meeting other millions and getting acquainted, so if the premise is true, we ought all to love each other like one big blessed family.

Instead, we hate each other like the devil. It is true that all over the world the nations are hating each other in startling, record-breaking measure.

I will mention another contradiction that is all too apparent. Our educators and sociologists told us that all we had to do was allow the teaching of sexual education in the schools and all of our vexing sexual problems in society would disappear.

Is it not a strange anomaly that the generation that has been teaching and outlining more about sexual practices than any twenty-five generations combined did in the past is the generation that is the most rotten and perverted in sexual conduct?

And is it not strange, too, that the very generation that might expect to be atomized suddenly by overkill is the generation that is afraid to talk about the coming of the Lord and unwilling to discuss His gracious promises of deliverance and glorification?

You may not expect me to say it, but I will: what a bunch of weirdies we are! What a strange generation we are!

God has said that He would place a great premium on the holy, spiritual consistency of the Christian saints, but how inconsistent we are when we allow the devil and our own carnality to confuse and mix us up so that we will be diverted from patient waiting for His appearing!

So, we live between two mighty events—that of His incarnation, death, and resurrection, and that of His ultimate appearing and the glorification of those He died to save. This is the interim time for the saints—but it is not a vacuum. He has given us much to do and He asks for our faithfulness.

In the meantime, we are zealous of good works, living soberly, righteously, godly in this present world, looking unto Him and His promise. In the midst of our lives, and between the two great mountain peaks of God's acts in the world, we look back and remember, and we look forward and hope! As members of His own loving fellowship, we break the bread and drink the wine. We sing His praise and we pray in His Name, remembering and expecting!

JESUS—THE IMAGE OF GOD

*The Son is the radiance of God's glory and the
exact representation of his being,
sustaining all things by his powerful word.*

HEBREWS 1:3

I wish I could comprehend everything that the inspired Word is trying to reveal in the statement that Jesus, the eternal Son, is the "brightness of his glory, and the express image of his person" (Hebrews 1:3). This much I do know and understand: Jesus Christ is, Himself, God. As a believer and a disciple, I rejoice that the risen, ascended Christ is now my High Priest and Intercessor at the heavenly throne.

The writer to the Hebrews commands our attention with this descriptive, striking language:

> [God] hath in these last days spoken unto us
> by his Son . . . who being the brightness of his
> glory, and the express image of his person, and
> upholding all things by the word of his power.
> HEBREWS 1:2–3

We trust the Scriptures because we believe they are inspired—God-breathed. Because we believe them, we believe and confess that Jesus was very God of very God.

Nothing anywhere in this vast, complex world is as beautiful and as compelling as the record of the incarnation, the act by which God was made flesh to dwell among us in our own human history. This Jesus, the Christ of God, who made the universe and who sustains all things by His powerful word, was a tiny babe among us. He was comforted to sleep when He whimpered in His mother's arms. Great, indeed, is the mystery of godliness.

Yet, in this context, some things strange and tragic have been happening in recent years within Christianity. For one, some ministers have advised their congregations not to be greatly concerned if theologians dispute the virgin birth of Jesus. The issue, they say, is not important. For another thing, some professing Christians are saying they do not want to be pinned down as to what they really believe about the uniqueness and reality of the deity of Jesus, the Christ.

We live in a society where we cannot always be sure that traditional definitions still hold. But I stand where I always have stood. And the genuine believer, no matter where he may be found in the world, humbly but surely is convinced about the person and position of Jesus Christ. Such a believer lives with calm and confident assurance that Jesus Christ is truly God and that He is everything the inspired writer said He is. He is "the brightness of his glory, and the express image of his person" (Hebrews 1:3). This view of Christ in Hebrews harmonizes with and supports what Paul said of Jesus when he described Him as "the image of the invisible God, the firstborn of every creature" (Colossians 1:15), in whom "dwelleth all the fulness of the Godhead bodily" (2:9).

Bible-believing Christians stand together on this. They may have differing opinions about the mode of baptism, church polity, or the return of the Lord. But they agree on the deity of the eternal Son. Jesus Christ is of one substance with the Father—begotten, not created (Nicene Creed). In our defense of this truth we must be very careful and very bold—belligerent, if need be.

The more we study the words of our Lord Jesus Christ when He lived on earth among us, the more certain we are about who He is. Some critics have protested, "Jesus did not claim to be God, you know. He only said He was the Son of Man."

It is true that Jesus used the term *Son of Man* frequently. If I can say it reverently, He seemed proud or at least delighted that He was a man, the Son of Man. But He testified boldly, even among those who were His sworn enemies, that He was God. He said with great forcefulness that He had come from the Father in heaven and that He was equal with the Father.

We know what we believe. Let no one with soft words and charming persuasion argue us into admission that Jesus Christ is any less than very God of very God.

THE WONDERS OF GOD DECLARED

No one has ever seen God, but the one and only Son, who is himself God and is in closest relationship with the Father, has made him known.

JOHN 1:18

Now the mystery of atonement had to be performed. Why in the Old Testament did the priest go behind the veil to perform the ritual of atonement and then come out from behind the veil? It was God saying, in beautiful symbolism, that there would be a day when another priest, with other blood, should enter into a realm where the mind of man could never penetrate, and there in a mystery too deep and dark and wonderful for man to understand, all alone with none to help him. Not David, not Abraham, not Paul—no one. Alone in the silence and the darkness he should make atonement for sin.

And that is what happened. God stepped back and allowed Him to die. But briefly and quickly, His heart was joined again to the love of God, for three days later He was raised from the dead and later ascended to the right hand of God the Father Almighty. And one day He shall come to judge the quick and the dead.

Now consider the closing line: "has made him known." What has Jesus declared about God? There are profundities that He could never declare, there are depths that He could never declare. But there are some things He could declare and did and does. He could declare God's holy being and, above all, for us poor sinners, He declared God's love and mercy. So He has set Him forth, and Jesus Christ tells us in His tender, human being, that God has a care for us.

I remember hearing years ago of four or five sons who had been reared in a home, and the old folks were wordless. They did not say much; they did not show much affection. Nobody did. And the boys didn't. After they were babies, they quit kissing their parents and quit using words of affection and grew to be strong men, and married and separated and got away. They seldom came home and seldom wrote. And when Mother's time had about come, they sent for the boys. They said if they wanted to see her, come. They came, all of them—big, fine fellows now, each with his own home and his own business and job. As they stood around her bed, one of them said, "Mother, we want you to know that you've meant a lot to us boys. We haven't been unappreciative. We've loved you, and we thank you."

And then they separated and when they were gone from her, she turned and said to someone by her side, "Oh, if they had only told me before. These years I've wondered if I had meant anything to them. These years I thought I had failed them. Now they tell me, 'We're so thankful.' If they had only told me earlier."

You know it is possible to feel a lot that you don't tell. It is possible to have fine intentions that you never make known. And how easy it might have been for God to have loved us and never told us, to have been merciful toward us and never revealed it. But the Scripture says that nobody ever saw God but the only begotten Son. Some translations say, "the only begotten God," who is "in the bosom of the Father." He has told us. He came to tell us what the silence never told us. He came to tell us what Moses could not even tell us. He came to tell us that God cares and God loves and God has a plan and God's carrying out that plan. And before it all is finished there will be a multitude—redeemed, out of every tongue and tribe and nation—that no man can number. That's what He told us.

He revealed God's being, love, grace, mercy, good intention, redemptive intention, saving intention. He gave it to us. Here it is. It is ours! Now we have only to turn and believe and accept and take and follow, and it all is ours.

LIFE AND LIGHT TO ALL HE BRINGS

I am the light of the world. Whoever follows me will never walk in darkness, but will have the light of life.

JOHN 8:12

This is the message we have heard from him and declare to you: God is light; in him there is no darkness at all.

1 JOHN 1:5

Here is the wonder of the nature of God: God is light, and in Him is no darkness at all. This is the wonder of life and light: the Scriptures mix up and do not try to keep separated *light* and *life*. "Light and life to all He brings, risen with healing in His wings." When that was written, theology was written, for life and light are one. This means that eternal life is also the light, the light of every man that cometh into the world. And I suppose that there is something deeper than morals here.

A great German theologian a generation ago wrote a book that has become very famous in learned circles. And in that book he declares that the idea of holiness goes back to personality. That you think of the holiness of God as a strange thing before you think of the person of God. I think he is right. I am quite sure he is right, and he says that the idea of purity is not the first idea of holiness. The first idea that comes to the mind, or that came to the mind, when the word *holy* was suggested was not the thought of being pure, but the idea of being greater than, higher than, other than, beyond, different from—in its self-sufficiency, uncreated substance of life. It is *that* without a pronoun, *that* without a personal pronoun, *that*—and then we attribute purity and holiness to God.

So when God says, "Be holy, because I am holy" (1 Peter 1: 16 NIV), He's talking about moral purity, He's talking about spiritual cleanness. But beyond that, in the back of that, and prior to that is the solemn, indescribable something that cannot be put into words: that there exists a nature, a substance in the universe that is life and light, and it is a thing, and it is *that*. But it also has personality and, that personality is God. And the wonder of this passage in John is the nature of God. God is light. God is life. And in Him is no darkness at all.

GOD'S BEST GIFT

. . . Christ loved us and gave himself up for us as a
fragrant offering and sacrifice to God . . .

EPHESIANS 5:2

God's gifts are many; His best gift is one. It is the gift
of Himself. Above all gifts, God desires most to
give Himself to His people. Our nature being what it is,
we are the best fitted of all creatures to know and enjoy
God. "For Thou madest us for Thyself, and our heart is
restless, until it repose in Thee" (from *The Confessions of
St. Augustine*).

When God told Aaron, "Thou shalt have no inheritance
in their land, neither shalt thou have any part among
them: I am thy part and thine inheritance among the
children of Israel" (Numbers 18:20), He in fact promised

a portion infinitely above all the real estate in Palestine and all the earth thrown in. To possess God—this is the inheritance ultimate and supreme.

There is a sense in which God never gives any gift except He gives Himself with it. The love of God, what is it but God giving Himself in love?

The mercy of God is but giving Himself in mercy, and so with all other blessings and benefits so freely showered upon the children of atonement. Deep within all divine blessing is the Divine One Himself dwelling as in a sanctuary.

Absalom dwelt two full years in Jerusalem and saw not the king's face, though the king was his own father. Are there not many in the kingdom of God who have no awareness of God, who seem not to know that they have the right to sit at the King's table and commune with the King? This is an evil that I have seen under the sun, and it is a hard and grievous burden.

To know God, this is eternal life; this is the purpose for which we are and were created. The destruction of our God-awareness was the master blow struck by Satan in the dark day of our transgression.

To give God back to us was the chief work of Christ in redemption. To impart Himself to us in personal experience is the first purpose of God in salvation. To bring acute God-awareness is the best help the Spirit brings in sanctification. All other steps in grace lead up to this.

Were we allowed but one request, we might gain at a stroke all things else by praying one all-embracing prayer:

Thyself, Lord! Give me Thyself and I can want no more.

PREPARING FOR THE BRIDEGROOM

All who have this hope in him purify themselves,
just as he is pure.

1 JOHN 3:3

Why is it that such a small proportion of Christian ministers ever feel the necessity to preach a sermon on the truth of His second coming? Why should pastors depend in this matter upon those who travel around the country with their colored charts and their object lessons and their curious interpretations of Bible prophecy?

Should we not dare to believe what the apostle John wrote, that "we shall be like him because we shall see him as he is"?

Beloved, we are the sons of God now, for our faith is in the Son of God, Jesus Christ! We believe in Him and we rest upon Him, and yet it doth not yet appear what we shall be; but we know that when He shall appear, when He shall be disclosed, we shall be like Him, for we shall see Him as He is!

Then, John says bluntly and clearly: "Every man that hath this hope in Him purifies himself, even as he is pure." Everybody! Everyone, he says! He singularizes it. Everyone that hath this hope in him purifies himself as He is pure!

Those who are expecting the Lord Jesus Christ to come and who look for that coming moment by moment and who long for that coming will be busy purifying themselves. They will not be indulging in curious specula-tions—they will be in preparation, purifying themselves!

It may be helpful to use an illustration here.

A wedding is about to take place and the bride is getting dressed. Her mother is nervous, and there are other relatives and helpers who are trying to make sure that the bride is dressed just right!

Why all this helpful interest and concern?

Well, the bride and those around her know that she is about to go out to meet the groom, and everything must be perfectly in order. She even walks cautiously so that nothing gets out of place in dress and veil. She is prepar-ing, for she awaits in loving anticipation and expectation the meeting with this man at the altar.

Now John says, through the Holy Ghost, that he that hath this hope in Him purifies and prepares himself. How? Even as He is pure!

The bride wants to be dressed worthy of the bridegroom, and so it is with the groom, as well!

Should not the church of Jesus Christ be dressed worthy of her bridegroom, even as He is dressed? Pure— even as He is pure?

We are assured that the appearing of Jesus Christ will take place. It will take place in His time. There are many who believe that it can take place soon—that there is not anything that must yet be done in this earth to make possible His coming.

It will be the greatest event in the history of the world, barring His first coming and the events of His death and resurrection.

We may well say that the next greatest event in the history of the world will be "the appearing of Jesus Christ: whom having not seen, we love; in whom, though now we see him not, yet believing, we rejoice with joy unspeakable and full of glory!"

The world will not know it, but he that hath this hope in him will know it for he has purified himself even as Christ is pure!

REFERENCES

WEEK 1

Day 1—The Lost Presence: A. W. Tozer, *Christ the Eternal Son* (Camp Hill, PA: Christian Publications, 1982; repr. Chicago: WingSpread Publishers, 2010), 13–15. / **Day 2—Bridging the Gulf:** A. W. Tozer, "The Word Became Flesh—The Mystery of It" (sermon, Southside Alliance Church, Chicago, December 20, 1953). / **Day 3—God Manifested in Flesh:** Tozer, *Christ the Eternal Son*, 17–19. / **Day 4—What the Advent Established:** A. W. Tozer, *The Set of the Sail* (Camp Hill, PA: Christian Publications, 1986; repr. Camp Hill, PA: WingSpread Publishers, 2009), 149–152. / **Day 5—The Meaning of Christmas:** A. W. Tozer, *The Warfare of the Spirit* (Camp Hill, PA: Christian Publications, 1993; repr. Chicago: WingSpread Publishers, 2006) 95–98. / **Day 6—Lukewarm about Christ's Return:** A. W. Tozer, *Born after Midnight*, (Camp Hill, PA: Christian Publications, 1959; repr. Chicago: Moody Publishers, 2015), 158–160. / **Day 7—Taking Up Humanity:** Tozer, "The Word Became Flesh—The Mystery of It" (sermon).

WEEK 2

Day 8—Light for the Darkness: A. W. Tozer, *Jesus Is Victor* (Camp Hill, PA: Christian Publications, 1989; repr. Camp Hill, PA: WingSpread Publishers, 2010), 7–9. / **Day 9—The Redemptive Plan:** Tozer, *Christ the Eternal Son*, 58–60. / **Day 10—Our Anticipation: Jesus the Victor!:** Tozer, *Jesus Is Victor*, 4–7. / **Day 11—The Logic of the Incarnation:** A. W. Tozer, *The Next Chapter After the Last* (Camp Hill, PA: Christian Publications, 1987; repr. Camp Hill, PA: WingSpread Publishers, 2010), 80–83. / **Day 12—Christ Came for All:** Tozer, *Christ the Eternal Son*, 101–103. / **Day 13—Christ—The Channel of Grace:** Tozer, *Christ the Eternal Son*, 21–23. / **Day 14—Let Us Prepare Now:** A. W. Tozer, *We Travel an Appointed Way* (Camp Hill, PA: Christian Publications, 1988; repr. Camp Hill, PA: WingSpread Publishers, 2010), 87–90.

WEEK 3

Day 15—The Glory of Christ: Tozer, "The Word Became Flesh—The Mystery of It" (sermon). / **Day 16—Just as He Went:** A. W. Tozer, *Tozer Speaks, Volume 2* (Camp Hill, PA: Christian Publications, 1994; repr. Camp Hill, PA: WingSpread Publishers, 2010), 151–152. / **Day 17—What We Have Received:** Tozer, *Christ the Eternal Son*, 27–29. / **Day 18—Trusting in God's Sovereignty:** Tozer, *Jesus Is Victor*, 1–4. / **Day 19—The Reasons He Came:** Tozer, *Christ the Eternal Son*, 103–105. / **Day 20—Christmas Reformation Long Overdue:** Tozer, *The Warfare of the Spirit*, 56–58. / **Day 21—Jesus—The Judge of Humanity:** A. W. Tozer, *Tozer Speaks, Volume 1* (Camp Hill, PA: Christian Publications, 1994; repr. Camp Hill, PA: WingSpread Publishers, 2010), 83–85.

WEEK 4

Day 22—Three Truths behind Christmas: A. W. Tozer, "The Birth of the Infant Lord" (sermon, Southside Alliance Church, Chicago, December 23, 1956). / **Day 23—Living in Between:** A. W. Tozer, *Who Put Jesus on the Cross?* (Camp Hill, PA: Christian Publications, 1976; repr. Camp Hill, PA: WingSpread Publishers, 2009), 167–170. / **Day 24—Jesus—The Image of God:** A. W. Tozer, *Jesus, Our Man in Glory* (Camp Hill, PA: Christian Publications, 1987; repr. Camp Hill, PA: WingSpread Publishers, 2009), 34–37. / **Day 25—The Wonders of God Declared:** Tozer, "The Word Became Flesh—The Mystery of It" (sermon). / **Day 26—Life and Light to All He Brings:** A. W. Tozer, "The Theology of Christmas" (sermon, Southside Alliance Church, Chicago, December 22, 1957). / **Day 27—God's Best Gift:** Tozer, *We Travel an Appointed Way*, 71–72. / **Day 28—Preparing for the Bridegroom:** A. W. Tozer, *Tozer Speaks, Volume 2*, 157–159.